culture
WISE

THINKING RIGHTLY ABOUT SEVEN SOCIETAL WRONGS

GRAHAM

P.O. Box 799070
Dallas, TX 75379
1-800-414-7693 (1-800-414-POWER)
jgraham@powerpoint.org
jackgraham.org

Unless otherwise indicated, Scripture verses quoted are
taken with permission from the English Standard Version.

—o-o-o—

contents

Chapter 1: Influencers Who Refuse to be Influenced   5

Chapter 2: Creation vs. Evolution   22

Chapter 3: The Sanctity of Human Life   31

Chapter 4: To Drink, or Not to Drink?   46

Chapter 5: Every Man's Battle, and How to Win   56

Chapter 6: Are Same-Sex Relationships Really the Same?   68

Chapter 7: Money, Money, Money   81

Chapter 8: Capital Punishment:
    What's Love Got to Do with It?   95

preface

One of my favorite books in the Bible is Proverbs, which is at its core simply a series of cautions and exhortations from father to son, warnings of common pitfalls and instruction for seeking wisdom in life. Each time I read those nuggets of gold, a pastoral burden heavies my heart. Being a pastor to people means I spend my days doing just that: *pastoring people.* It means my primary task is journeying with them, as they find their way toward truth. It means I help them negotiate cultural riptides, teaching them to swim a straight line amid societal trends that are twisted and harmful and sick. It means I invite them to a new level of engagement in the Christian life, in which they influence others for good.

All of us who have received the saving love of Jesus Christ know well the experience of having our sins blotted out. We know what it is to go from "lost" to "found," from far away to blissfully right at home. Yes, our sin was great, but God's grace proved greater still.

But even as we know how to receive the marvelous gifts of rescue and redemption and right-standing before a loving God, we remain perplexed regarding how to stand firm in that place when the ground all around us seems shifty, uncertain, and unsafe. We don't understand how to be *conduits of redemption* in a world that so desperately needs to be redeemed.

Which brings me to the purpose of this book.

Here, I've assembled seven subjects that seem to be causing the most heated debates today, including what the Bible has to say about them all. Certainly these are not the only issues in which serious-minded Christ followers should be well versed. But they are critical ones; and perhaps as we walk through the trends, the theologies, the various perspectives involved with each, you'll pick up patterns for right, godly thinking that will serve you well *whenever* in life you face wrongs.

Jack Graham
Plano, Texas
October 2012

1

influencers who refuse to be influenced

History bears testimony to an ebb-and-flow relationship between man and God, which impacts not just the human heart, but also entire communities, churches, cities, countries, and even continents. For instance, there was a time when Europe was an utterly pagan place. But then a wave of missionaries and evangelists brought with them the Gospel of Jesus Christ, the message of grace and acceptance and love, and Christianity swept beautifully across the land. Over time, however, the people fell away from the faith that had saved them, the culture digressed, and an entire continent fell headlong into secularism—society without any use for God. As I say, ebb, then flow, then ebb.

This same trend can be seen when we look at the United States of America: what was once a nation founded on Judeo-Christian principles has now become a secular society, a people who have little use for God.

While Jesus ministered here on earth, in the midst of real society facing real challenges, He told His followers that they were like "sheep among wolves" (Matthew 10:16). In order to survive, He continued, we would have to be wise as serpents and innocent as doves; we'd need to keep in mind that while we're to refrain at every turn from harming others, we live in a world that doesn't necessarily share that lack of ill-intent. We must be suspicious while somehow remaining sweet, because we're living among wolves. And wolves seek to devour.

Romans 1 aptly describes what a wolf-riddled culture looks like: "The wrath of God is revealed from heaven against all ungodliness and unrighteousness of men, who suppress the truth in unrighteousness, because what may be known of God is manifest in them, for God has shown it to them. For since the creation of the world His invisible attributes are clearly seen, being understood by the things that are made, even His eternal power and Godhead, so that they are without excuse" (vv. 18-20).

A few verses down, we read the stunning, sobering implications of secularized society: "Therefore God also gave them up to uncleanness, in the lusts of their hearts, to dishonor their bodies among themselves, who exchanged the truth of God for the lie, and worshipped and served the creature rather than the Creator, who is blessed forever. For this reason God gave them up to vile passions. For even their women exchanged the natural use of what is against nature. Likewise also the men, leaving the natural use of the women, burned in their lust for one another, men with men committing what is shameful, and receiving in themselves the penalty of their error which was due. And even as they did not like to retain God in their knowledge, God gave them over to a debased mind to do those things which are not fitting" (vv. 24-28).

And to what habits does God "give them over to"? Verses 29 through 32 spell it out in graphic detail: sexual immorality, wickedness, covetousness, maliciousness, envy, murder, strife, deceit, and evil-mindedness. Furthermore, we learn that these people, the ones whom God is "giving over" are quite deserving of the punishment they face. According to the same passage of Scripture, they are "whisperers, back biters, haters of God, violent, proud, boasters, inventors of evil things, disobedient to parents, undiscerning, untrustworthy, unloving, unforgiving, unmerciful."

Sounds familiar, doesn't it? The description reads like the cover of the *Dallas Morning News* on any given Sunday. Indeed, you and I are living among the "un-generation"— people who are undiscerning, untrustworthy, unloving, unforgiving, and unmerciful. The result of this unlovely living is a society that is first and foremost *twisted sexually*. People no longer honor God's plan for marriage. They no longer find fulfillment within the confines of "man and wife." They indulge their lusts, they prize experimentation, they treat sexual encounters as base bodily functions instead of honoring them as God-given gifts to prize.

What once embarrassed and shamed us now does not faze us. What used to slink down dark, back alleyways now struts along the main streets of our hearts. May God have mercy on us all.

This type of living also produces a society that is *twisted spiritually*. We indulge our wickedness long enough, and we eventually become anti-God. We glaze over at the news of the Gospel—that Jesus' blood really does cover our every sin. We step away from the truths of salvation, figuring we're better off going it alone. We eye the Bible with foolhardy skepticism, finding it a book of fables and nothing more. We do our level best to get rid of God, even as our very

> We while away our days and lives, chasing counterfeit answers to God, but in the end, science and business and vain pleasures can do nothing to scratch the angry itch in our souls.

nature cries out for Him. We while away our days and lives, chasing counterfeit answers to God, but in the end, science and business and vain pleasures can do nothing to scratch the angry itch in our souls.

Secularized living yields a *twisted morality*, too. Immorality winds up giving way to amorality, a place where degradation and promiscuity proudly reign.

Certainly, it's important for us as Christ's followers to keep our distance from such characteristics—being twisted sexually, spiritually, morally—but God expects still more. He says we must also speak out against these habits; we must *actively disapprove of these trends*. Romans 1:32 says it this way: "Though they know God's righteous decree that those who practice such things deserve to die, they not only do them but give approval to those who practice them" (emphasis added).

Those of us who believe in Jesus and have staked our very lives on His saving grace are called to stand against all forms of godlessness. We are called to help our society once again pursue God. But how do we get that done?

Be Savory, as Salt

One day, Jesus looked into the eyes of His disciples, who were seated before Him on the side of a mountain, and reassured them that it actually is possible to live as citizens of His kingdom in a fallen and fractured world. "You are the salt of the earth!" He said. "You're here to be salt-seasoning that brings out the God-flavors of this earth. If you lose your saltiness, how will people taste godliness? You've lost your usefulness and will end up in the garbage" (Matthew 5:13, The Message).

Jesus may as well have said, "Listen, I know you'll meet a lot of tasteless people, hear a lot of tasteless jokes, and see a lot of tasteless things, down here on planet Earth. But don't lose heart! As you fulfill your mission to honor God with your life, you'll bring tastefulness back in style. Keep in mind as you walk through life that you have far more influence than you know."

> As you fulfill your mission to honor God with your life, you'll bring tastefulness back in style.

The message was aimed at us, too. Think of it: when Jesus himself delivered those words, He was a young man, barely thirty years of age; He had been raised in a two-bit town called Nazareth; He was the earthly son of a commoner, Joseph the carpenter; and He made His living as an itinerate preacher. And yet He possessed more influence than the world has ever known.

Similarly, we tend to think of Jesus' disciples as saints—and indeed, they rose to great heights as their Master empowered and shaped them, emboldened them and increased their reach. But these were ordinary men! They were fishermen and tax collectors who turned the world upside-down, not because they were especially gifted or famous, but because they'd had an encounter with God.

The same can be true of us. We can be average Joes and Janes, going about our average daily lives, and yet God lays His hand upon us and declares us fit to utterly change the world. The most powerful agent of change in this world is not the government, the military, entertainers or leaders of industry. No, the most powerful agent of change is Christ's church, people committed to doing His will.

> We can be average Joes and Janes, going about our average daily lives, an yet God lays His hand upo us and declares us fit to utterly change the world.

Salt Preserves and Protects

So, what does "being salt" have to do with it?

When Jesus told His disciples—and us—that we are the "salt of the earth," He reinforced our role as those who preserve and protect the crown of His creation, His people. The salt of Jesus' time was full of minerals and had an unmatched ability to preserve and protect valuable food in the days before refrigeration and the practice of packing with ice were available. If a fisherman reeled in a draught of fish, for example, and needed to transport it from Capernaum to Jerusalem—a distance of about 120 miles—he would be sure to salt it down so that it didn't spoil en route. He would rub the salt into the flesh of the fish, penetrating it, preserving it, protecting it.

This is how we are to live.

We are to penetrate our culture with grace and truth so that those living this life beside us are not spoiled by sin en route.

Now, it's possible you're mumbling a quick defense, along the lines of, "That's well and good for you, Pastor, but I choose to keep my faith private, so I don't risk offending anyone."

It's a posture that is not only ignorant; it's highly arrogant, too.

It is ignorant to believe that a decaying world will somehow spontaneously start to produce life. Death produces more death; decay only leads to decay. In spite of scientific achievements and technological advancements aplenty, the world is in more trouble than ever today. For us to believe that our "silent witness" somehow will reverse the debilitating trends of immorality and amorality in our society is foolishness. Only life produces life, and eternal life is what our culture most needs.

> Only life produces life, and eternal life is what our culture most needs.

———o-0-o———

But there's arrogance here we must address too. To assert that somehow, by our quietly noble lives and silent, steady stream of good works, we can convert anyone from godlessness to full devotion represents self-importance of the very worst kind. Yes, we will be known as Jesus' followers by things such as love and kindness and fruit. But equally true is that we are called to share the Gospel message in a manner that plainly points people directly to God. Our faith is to be personal. But *private*? That it's not.

Salt Seasons and Stings

A second aspect to Jesus' metaphor is that salt also seasons and stings.

> When Jesus told us t be "salty," He was ir essence saying, "Let your life make other thirsty for God!"

You've likely had the experience of being in a movie theater with a belly full of salty, buttered popcorn. The only thing you can think about is washing it down with an oversize Coke, which is why movie theaters can get away with charging five bucks for a soda that costs them mere pennies to make. But the point is this: salt makes us thirsty. When Jesus told us to be "salty," He was in essence saying, "Let your life make others thirsty for God!"

We are to craft our lives in such a way that our thoughts, our habits, our actions and reactions make people who know us simply crave God. We're to experience the abundance Christ offers and then to share that true life with others we meet.

Clearly, this encouragement from our Master implies that we'll actually hang out with a few unconvinced folks. Jesus modeled being a friend to sinners, but many of His followers refuse to follow suit. Instead, we congregate in big saltshakers known as sanctuaries, huddled in fear of a big, bad world. Sure, we look good in there, all crystalized and gleaming white. But salty people don't need seasoning! It's the bland world outside that needs our salt. So yes, we are to be in the world in order to season it, but we're also to deliver a sting.

Perhaps you've known the agony of swimming in the ocean with a fresh cut on your face or leg. Maybe you sliced your skin shaving that morning and completely forgot about the gash, until you dove into that body of saltwater and were quickly reminded as you winced in pain. Salt can sting. It's true in the physical realm; it's true in the spiritual realm, too.

If you follow Jesus long enough, you will encounter people who don't appreciate hearing truth. It's a stinging rebuke to their godless life, and inside, they wince in pain. But still, we must proclaim the message Jesus has asked us to proclaim. All are sinners in need of grace. All must trust Christ to find true life.

We are called to be salt—and not sugar!—in our world. We are called to season and to sting.

Salt Cleanses and Heals

Let me give you one more duo, about living the "salty" life. In addition to preserving and protecting, to seasoning and providing a sting, salt also is known as a powerful agent for *cleansing and healing wounds*.

If you've ever had a sore throat, then you know that one of the quickest, most surefire ways to soothe the passage and relieve the pain is by gargling saltwater. Similarly, we are to look for parts of our homes, our communities, our cities, our world in need of soothing, in need of relief, and we are to be *salt* that cleanses, that heals.

I see brokenness and fallenness and agony all around, and I know you must see it, too. But we can take heart that God has left us here, to be channels of change for our world. By our saltiness, we can help mend what is broken. We can lift up what has been laid down. We can bring to life what has been massacred. We can be a blessing each day of our lives. This is what Jesus meant that day, when He called His followers to live as salt.

> y our saltiness,
> ve can help
> nend what is
> roken.

Shine Brightly, as Lights

On that same day, on that same hillside, during that same conversation with His wide-eyed disciples, Jesus offered another metaphor for living, building on the "salt" speech he'd just delivered. "Not only are you to be the salt of the earth," our Master conveyed, "but also, you're to be *light*." Here are His verbatim words, from Matthew 5:14:

> *You are the light of the world. A city set on a hill cannot be hidden. Nor do people light a lamp and put it under a basket, but on a stand, and it gives light to all in the house. In the same way, let your light shine before others, so that they may see your good works and give glory to your Father who is in heaven.*

When ancient civilizations were formed, cities often were built along hillsides. Armies would attack and conquer and enforce their rule over a particular city by rebuilding right on top of the previous city's structures. Over time, you'd have city upon city upon city, stacked higher and higher each time, to show onlookers who was in charge.

There's a spiritual implication for us here. As followers of Jesus Christ, we are to have a visible presence that boldly glorifies God, who rules over all. We are to stand proudly, as a city on a hill. We are to shine brightly, as a candle positioned high on a stand. Our lives are to cast a glow to the watching world that confirms we've been in the presence of God. Let's look at how this gets done.

Be Conspicuous

First, we are to be *conspicuous*. Rather than living a covert Christian life, we are to wear our association with Jesus with confidence, remembering that people all around us are wandering, in search of something—or

> Rather than living a cover Christian life, we are to wea our associatic with Jesus witl confidence...

Someone—to soothe their souls. We cannot help point people to faith in Christ unless we're known as Christ followers ourselves.

Frequently I have someone from our church approach me and bemoan their work or school environment, regaling me with all the sordid details of their colleague's wayward lives: "Pastor, you don't *know* how lucky you are, to get to be here at the church all day! The language I have to put up with at the place where I work ... it's just a dark, dark place."

What these people fail to recognize is that the place of darkness where they find themselves could be illuminated *if they'd shine their light.* Their office or school isn't their punishment; it's their divinely given ministry, where they can glorify God.

> We're to serve as lighthouses that guide people home, that dispel darkness and offer much-needed hope.

The light of Jesus—in your eyes, in your heart, in your spirit, in your reaction when a colleague does you wrong—will attract people to you. We're to serve as lighthouses that guide people home, that dispel darkness and offer much-needed hope.

Be Consistent

Second, we are to be *consistent* in our followership of Christ. I often refer jokingly to inconsistent believers as "mugwumps"—they're fence-straddlers who have their mug on one side and their wumps on the other! They never quite fully devote themselves to the will and the ways of Christ.

Too many churches today are full of mugwumps. They say they love God and are committed to serving him alone, but in reality they live in a manner totally indistinguishable from the way people far from God choose to live. Case in point: Professional pollsters have long told us that the divorce rate among members of the church is nearly identical to the divorce rate of those outside the church. We make compromises in life and then act shocked when our light doesn't shine as brightly as it once did. I'm not encouraging self-righteousness here; I'm simply suggesting that our testimonies would be far more effective if we'd ask God to remove *anything* inconsistent from our lives.

Be Consumed

Third, we are to be utterly *consumed* by the light of Jesus in our lives. John the Baptist said it this way: "I must decrease, but he must increase" (John 3:30). We make *more* room for the Holy Spirit's work in our lives by making *less* room for ourselves. Because when our light shines as

Jesus intends, prompting us to love well and do well in our world, people will be absolutely compelled to glorify not us, but *the Father in heaven above*.

Wherever it is you find yourself, God intends for you to be salt and light *right there*. "Never allow the thought, *I'm of no use where I am*," Oswald Chambers once wrote. "You certainly are no use where you are not." May we recommit ourselves to influencing the world around us, instead of being wholly influenced by it.

creation vs. evolution

The first chapter of the first book of the Bible has caused great debate throughout history, all centered on this question: *Did God make man or did man make God?*

In 1859 Charles Darwin, at the time an eminent scientist, published "The Origin of Species,"[1] a scientific theory that populations are not created by a divine Creator, but rather evolve over the course of generations via natural selection. The premise, according to Darwin himself, is this: "All animals and plants are descended from one prototype. All organisms start from a common origin; from some such low and intermediate forms, both animals and plants may have been developed and all the organic things which have ever lived on the earth may be descended from one primordial form."[2]

According to this theory, all higher forms of life (which includes you and me) have evolved from lower forms of life;

[1] Original title: On the Origin of Species by Means of Natural Selection, or the Preservation of Favoured Races in the Struggle for Life. [2] p.523

we've shifted from simple organisms to complex organisms. Life began with primitive protozoa being transmuted to worms, and worms became fish, and fish became amphibians, and amphibians became reptiles, and reptiles became birds, and birds became mammals, and mammals became men.

By the fortuitous concourse of atoms, by selective chance or natural selection, by spontaneous generation, *everything* that we have now, according to evolutionary theory, came into being. Based on what proponents of this argument say, frogs really *can* become princes.

But this is not at all what God says.

"In the beginning," Genesis 1:1 says, "God created the heavens and the earth." Later in the same chapter, we read that God said, "Let the earth bring forth living creatures according to their kinds" (v. 24); and, still later, that He said, "Let us make man in our image, after our likeness. And let them have dominion over the fish of the sea and over the birds of the heavens and over the livestock and over all the earth and over every creeping thing that creeps on the earth" (v. 26).

In other words, according to Scripture, *God made it all.*

Populations did not spontaneously appear and then evolve over time, from one species to another. No, populations arrived by the spoken word of God—intentionally designed, supernaturally created,

> When God made you
> He breathed into
> you the breath of life,
> in an *instant* declaring
> you a living soul.

divineley loved. When God made you, He breathed into you the breath of life, in an *instant* declaring you a living soul. And that soul will live for eternity—either with God in heaven someday, or else apart from God in hell. You and I need to know this. Our friends and family members need to know this. Every person walking the planet needs to know this crucial truth, which is why I'm so passionate about spreading the Word.

In case you are afforded an opportunity to explain the differences between creation and evolution, let's look at the three primary reasons that the theory of evolution falls flat on its face. First: there is the *problem of logic*.

The Problem of Logic

Evolution theorizes that nothing times nobody equals everything. And despite the theory's widespread acceptance, despite the fact that our kids are having it shoveled into their mouths, courtesy of biased textbooks and ill-informed teachers, nothing times nobody *never* equals everything. Even scientists who once espoused evolutionary theory are starting to back away. Consider Dr. Newton Tahmisian, a physicist for the Atomic Energy Commission, who says, "Scientists who go about teaching that evolution is a fact of life are great con men, and the story they are telling people may be the greatest hoax ever. In explaining evolution, we do not have one iota of fact."[3]

Scientists such as Tahmisian are backing away because they simply cannot cross the bridge of the origin of life. If all of life came from one singular primordial amoeba, then where did that primordial amoeba come from? From whence did that tiny germ of life arise?

All evolutionists can do is guess. "The first germ of life came to earth riding a meteor from outer space!" they cheer. Or, as one MIT scientist supposes, "a prehistoric visitor from outer space left his garbage can on planet Earth, and from that garbage, life was produced." He went on to say that we should leave our garbage cans on other planets to help life get started elsewhere.

—————————o

[3] http://www.soulwinners.com.au/8.html

How true it is that it takes more faith to believe evolutionary theory than to simply believe the Word of God. One Princeton University professor has said that to suggest that life happened by accident has about the same probability of suggesting that a Webster's Unabridged Dictionary came about from an explosion in a printing factory.

> ... it takes more faith to believe evolutionary theory than to simply believe the Word of God

I happen to agree with that professor.

A second logic-bridge that evolutionists cannot cross is that of the fixity of the species. Genesis 1 is careful to confirm that God brought forth animals and man "according to their kinds." In other words, transmutation between species was never part of God's design, and it has never been demonstrated by man. A rose may have numerous varieties, but still, it is a rose. A rose has never produced a banana. Roses always produce *roses*.

Yes, archaeologists have located millions of fossil records throughout history, but never once has a transitional form be found. Never. Once. Not one transmutation can be proven, which isn't to say we're simply missing a link. It's to say the entire *chain* has somehow disappeared. Again, the logic just is not there.

The Problem of Morality

I also reject evolutionary theory on the basis of *morality*. If man is but a higher animal—a modified monkey, as it were—then man is living in a morass of meaninglessness. We're nothing more than a genetic glitch, waiting to evolve. If there is no God, there is no need for morality, which reflects the righteousness He prizes and possesses and promotes among the crown of His creation. And based on empirical evidence, when you begin teaching people that they came from animals, it isn't long before they start acting like animals.

I read recently of a group of young people who committed themselves to moral purity by taking a pledge during a youth conference. In the article, a spokesperson from the liberal organization Planned Parenthood was quoted as saying that it was "unreasonable" to expect young people to be morally pure today. According to recent trends, more than 70 percent of high-school seniors have had sexual intercourse; in essence, this spokesperson was saying, "So, why bother?"

I found it interesting that an adjacent article in this particular newspaper showed the results of a recent Gallup poll, in which more than 70 percent of today's young people don't believe in the literal truth of the Bible. Do you see what I see? When there is no God, when there is no authority on truth, when there is no accountability for living uprightly, we give ourselves over to a meaningless life.

The Problem of Theology

Finally, I reject the theory of evolution for *theological* reasons. The Word of God simply doesn't endorse evolution, regardless of how many people try to bend various Scriptures that way.

British author H.G. Wells, who himself was not a Christ follower, once astutely observed that, "If all animals and man evolved, then there were no first parents, no paradise, and no fall. And if there was no fall, then the entire historic fabric of Christianity, the story of the first sin, and the reason for the atonement, which is the reason for the cross, collapses like a house of cards!"

Mr. Wells had it right.

The Bible teaches us that God created man supernaturally and substantively, He placed that man in an environment in which man sinned and rebelled and fell into depravity, and that because of His great love He provided His one and only Son, Jesus Christ, to pay the debt that rebellion incurred. Man did not *evolve*, for if this were the case, man still would be evolving. And a quick scan of our societal horizon tells us that, if anything, we're *devolving*, not evolving. Yes, we are greater in terms of intellectual capacity and technology, but morally, we are spiraling down.

Which is why we so desperately need the new life afforded by Christ alone.

The Bible says that when God created the heavens and the earth, He did so from a formless reality. Darkness was on the face of the deep. A huge void was all there was. But from this void, God spoke *life* into existence. He continues to do this today.

> , huge void
> was all there
> was. But from
> his void, God
> spoke *life* into
> xistence.

Despite man's dulled conscience, his life now dead in sin, his understanding darkened, God whispers, "I'm ready to give you life!"

The moment you receive Christ into your heart, the light and life and love of God comes to reside there. That is salvation, in a nutshell, and that is what ensures your eternity with God.

So, yes, it is critical to know of our origin, to understand how we arrived on this big, blue, beautiful planet. But equally important—perhaps more important still—is grasping where we're headed, based on what we do with Christ.

Nothing plus nobody has never equaled everything. But your desperation plus God's divine intervention will always equal everlasting life.

the sanctity of human life

Tiny wonder, little human,
Lying still, your hands outstretched.
I wonder what you might have been,
I wonder what you might have done.
Sixteen weeks - that's all you lived
Until they wrenched you out of the womb
To lie unattended, gasping, stunned,
A plastic bag to be your tomb.
They weigh your form, record its length;
Perfect tissue, soulless, mute.
Your life, so small, was still too much.
You died without one loving touch.
Spark of existence, now no more,
Snuffed out by those who came before.
I wonder what you might have been,
I wonder what you might have done.[4]

I n the late 1980s, eighteen-month-old Jessica McClure fell into a twenty-two-foot well in the backyard of a West Texas home, sparking a nationwide media frenzy centered for more than fifty hours on freeing "Baby Jessica." But the well was only eight inches in diameter; how were rescue workers supposed to get her out?

[4] Dr. David C. Thompson composed this poem after witnessing an abortion

People all across the United States prayed for her, wept for her, sent their high hopes for a dramatic rescue to her fear-stricken parents. As a nation, we were determined that the little girl get out *alive*.

And she did, in the end. Through technology called waterjet cutting, the toddler's body was extracted from the narrow pipe, and with only minimal bruises and injuries to report.

Life is precious, isn't it. There are thousands of stories all around us, testifying to the value of human life. Just as when Baby Jessica was trapped inside that well, something overwhelms us when life is endangered; we fight with all we have to see it spared.

... something overwhelms us when life endangered we fight with all we have see it spared

Which is why it was so interesting to me that even as an entire nation begged God all those years ago to protect one toddler's life, we carried out the murders of thousands of babies in their mothers' wombs.

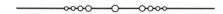

Since the historic *Roe vs. Wade* decision in 1973, which lifted many state and federal restrictions on abortion in the United States, there have been more than 48 million babies killed in our country—more than one million per year; more than three thousand per day; more than one hundred per hour; *nearly twenty abortions every ten minutes.*[5]

There have been no trials for these deaths, no jurors gathered to listen to evidence and decide those babies' fate, no one present at all to speak up for them, to save them from certain execution. There was only death—cruel, inhumane death—some whose lives were cut short by suction, which tore them limb by limb. Some who were surgically scraped from their mother's womb. Others who writhed in agony following a searing salt-solution injection. Still more who were removed from their mothers' bodies and left on a table to die.

This is no "minor surgery" we're talking about. This is the weightiest of all possible procedures because it ends the life of an innocent soul.

Abortion is Legally Wrong

In thinking about the subject of abortion and whether it

—o

[7] http://www.all.org/article/index/id/MjQ0NQ

should be allowed in this country, it is not overstatement to say that *abortion is legally wrong.* The issue of abortion has never been voted on through a duly appointed process or election in the United States of America. No legislature has ever passed a law for abortion. What has happened, however, is a fair amount of activity at the judicial level, in our country's courts, most notably, in *Roe vs. Wade.*

On January 22, 1973, the Supreme Court, understanding that laws may be made independently of the Constitution based on the necessity of the moment, voted seven to two that a mother may abort her child, as long as three requirements were present: the baby must still live inside the mother's body; the mother must desire the baby's abortion; and a doctor must be willing to perform the abortion. Officially, the law read this way: "A state is forbidden to prescribe or forbid abortion any time before birth if in the opinion of one licensed physician an abortion is necessary to preserve the life or health of the mother."

And it is in that last little phrase—"the health of the mother"— that Pandora's box was opened, allowing all sorts of evil to creep out. In defining "the health of the mother," courts have ruled that, "the medical judgment may be exercised in the light of all factors: physical, emotional, psychological, familial, and the woman's age relevant to the well-being of the patient. All of these factors may relate to the health of the mother."

So, if having the baby might bring stress, distress, psychological difficulty, or trauma of any sort; if having a baby might shroud the mother with the stigma of unwed motherhood; if in some way—*any* way—the mother's well-being could be jeopardized as a result of giving birth, then the abortion may be performed. And so, they are performed.

Women seeking abortions would ask, "Don't I have the right to do with my body whatever I choose to do?" And they have asked the question frequently enough and with sufficient passion that it has singlehandedly shifted the issue of abortion from an ethical, life-and-death consideration to one of personal rights, which happen to be protected by the 14th Amendment of the Constitution.

Part of the challenge to those of us among the "pro-life" camp is that women are human persons who possess rights that embryos or fetuses do not possess until their personhood can be established, which is generally held to be at around 24 weeks' gestation. Several Constitutional Amendments—not just the 14th—protect personhood and well-being, and pro-choice advocates are able to stake their claim on them all, in fighting for abortion as a legal course of action in this country.

This is where it is handy to know God's Word—specifically, Psalm 139. Verses 13 through 16 (The Message) read:

> *Oh yes, you shaped me first inside, then out;*
> *you formed me in my mother's womb.*
> *I thank you, High God—you're breathtaking!*
> *Body and soul, I am marvelously made!*
> *I worship in adoration—what a creation!*
> *You know me inside and out,*
> *you know every bone in my body;*
> *You know exactly how I was made, bit by bit,*
> *how I was sculpted from nothing into something.*
> *Like an open book, you watched me grow from conception*
> *to birth;*
> *all the stages of my life were spread out before you,*
> *The days of my life all prepared*
> *before I'd even lived one day.*

We are "fearfully and wonderfully made," some translations say, not upon birth, but beginning in the womb of our mothers. In the human body there are 30 trillion cells, letters of a divine alphabet that spell out unique characteristics of a brand new individual. Even a pea-sized fetus in the womb has everything necessary for determining eye color, hair color, skin type, facial features, personality, and intelligence.

> You and I are far more than "products of conception!" We are intricate, holy designs, fashioned by the Creator of the universe.

You and I are far more than "products of conception!" We are intricate, holy designs, fashioned by the Creator of the universe. And a baby inside the mother's womb is more than just a part of that mother's body. He or she also is a distinct, unique life, desperate to be born.

—o-o-o—O—o-o-o—

Following the landmark *Roe vs. Wade* decision, Judge Byron White, one of the two dissenting justices, said, "I find nothing in the language or history of the Constitution to support the

Court's judgment. The Court simply fashions and announces a new Constitutional right as an exercise of raw judicial power. The Court perhaps had authority to do what it did today, but in my view, its judgment is an improvident and extravagant exercise of the power of judicial review."[6]

He went on to make this strong assertion: "The Court, for the most part, sustains this position: during the period prior to the time the fetus becomes viable, the Constitution of the United States values the convenience, whim, or caprice of the putative mother more than the life or potential life of the fetus." [7]

To accommodate the culture of the times and the moral flagrancy of a desperate, self-focused people, the Court caved to pressure. We're reaping the awful effects still today.

Abortion is Medically Wrong

Abortion is legally wrong; it is also *medically* wrong. The backbone of modern medicine is the Hippocratic Oath, an oath all healthcare professionals take that swears them to practice medicine honestly and ethically. The oath itself is filled to overflowing with exhortations against abortion, namely, that practitioners treating patients do them "no harm," that they treat patients' children as

6 and 7 http://www.endroe.org/dissentswhite.aspx#_ftn2

their "own brother," and that they refuse to provide a woman a "pessary [or medical device] to provide an abortion."[8]

How far we as a society have drifted from medicine's origins. We simply must find our way back.

What Hippocrates understood was the medical evidence supporting the start of human life. Former United States Surgeon General C. Everett Coop once said, "We can find no point in time between the union of sperm and egg and the birth of an infant at which point we can say, 'this is not human life.' Medical evidence points to the fact that at early conception we have human life."

In a 1968 Harvard Medical School study aimed at determining clinical death, four criteria were examined. First, there must be no response to external stimuli; second, there must be a lack of deep-reflex action; third, there must be a lack of spontaneous movement and respiratory effect; and fourth, there must be a lack of brain activity. It probably goes without saying that a baby in the mother's womb fails the death-test in all four capacities. *Life* is in the womb!

Medically, abortion is wrong.

⁸ http://www.medterms.com/script/main/art.asp?articlekey=20909

Abortion is Psychologically Wrong

Furthermore, abortion is wrong *psychologically* because it denies the God-given instincts of precious would-be moms. Motherhood begins at conception; there is *automatically* a maternal tug on the heart. In fact, researcher Anne C. Speckhard, Ph.D, performed a study on the long-term manifestation of stress on women who had had abortions five to ten years prior, in which she discovered the following troubling trends:

> Motherhood begins at conception; there is *automatically* a maternal tug on the heart.

- 100 percent of these women reported feelings of sadness, regret, remorse, or a sense of loss
- 92 percent reported feelings of depression
- 92 percent reported feelings of guilt
- 89 percent reported fear that others would learn of their pregnancy and abortion experience
- 81 percent reported feelings of diminished self-worth
- 81 percent reported feelings of victimization
- 81 percent reported preoccupation with the characteristics of the aborted child
- 73 percent reported feelings of depressed effect or suppressed ability to experience pain

- 73 percent reported feelings of discomfort around small children
- 81 percent reported frequent crying
- 77 percent reported an inability to communicate with others concerning the pregnancy and abortion experience
- 73 percent reported flashbacks of the abortion experience
- 69 percent reported sexual inhibition
- 65 percent reported suicide ideation
- 61 percent reported increased alcohol use[9]

Ms. Speckhard's findings are hardly anecdotal. Trauma, trouble, disturbance, and distress are the unfortunate hallmarks of women who have made the decision to abort a child.

Abortion is Biblically Wrong

Finally, abortion is *biblically* wrong. *All* persons are uniquely created by God. All persons—including fetuses of *any* age.

All people have spiritual capability. All lives are sacred. All babies deserve the right to be born. We must be careful not to play god when it comes to opening and closing wombs.

[9] The Psycho-Social Aspects of Stress Following Abortion, Anne C. Speckhard, (Kansas City: Sheed and Ward, 1987).

The Bible says that we cannot break God's laws without suffering, and Proverbs 6 makes it clear that God hates hands that shed innocent blood. He prizes life and asks His followers to prize life, too. "I set before you life and death, blessing or cursing," Deuteronomy 30 says. "Choose life."

Righting Abortion's Wrongs

While nothing you and I can do will bring back the millions upon millions of babies who have been senselessly executed through the years, there are plenty of steps we can take to help mothers make a better choice from this point forward, things we can do to choose life over death, to help be a blessing instead of a curse.

We Can Be Informed

First, we can inform ourselves by reading the literature, studying the stats, having the conversations, engaging in this crisis as if it were our problem, too. Because it is.

We Can Work for Change

Second, we can work toward and pray for a constitutional amendment that forbids and prohibits abortion based on the fact that life is viable beginning at conception.

We Can Teach Morality in Our Homes and Churches

Third, we can take an active role in teaching morality in the home and the church. Sex education in most schools is highly biased, leaving out any semblance of moral or biblical teaching, which leaves the educating to us as parents. We must take responsibility for teaching our children to be moral individuals, who understand the purpose and place for sex, as a first step in reducing "unwanted" pregnancy rates and therefore reducing the demand for abortions.

> We must take responsibility for teaching our children to be moral individuals...

We Can Provide Alternatives

Next, we can provide alternatives for those women considering abortion. It is not useful to pontificate the evils of abortion if we are not willing to propose solutions for the real problems these moms face. Most every geographical area in this country is supported by some sort of crisis-pregnancy center that accepts either in-person volunteer support, donated supplies, or financial funding. These centers are designed to offer a compassionate response to those seeking abortion, by presenting alternatives, caring for practical needs, and offering support for women who choose to carry their babies to term, such as contact with adoption agencies.

We Can Ask God to Heal Our Land

Finally, we can pray, pray, pray, for God's presence, power, and peace to reign, in the lives of those wrestling with the decision and the aftereffects of abortion. God tells us in His Word that if His people will "humble themselves, and pray and seek my face and turn from their wicked ways, then I will hear from heaven and will forgive their sin and heal their land" (2 Chron. 7:14).

This is quite a promise! Complete healing, complete forgiveness, await us. But we must first uphold our end of the deal. We must first humble ourselves as a nation. We must diligently pray. We must passionately seek God's face. We must *turn from our wicked ways.*

> We must diligently pray. We must passionately seek God's face. We must *turn from our wicked ways*

We Can Choose Life Ourselves

Before taking any of the aforementioned actions, though, there is an all-important first step: God's grace is sufficient for any person, regardless of what that person has done, where that person has been, or how many abortions that person has had. But we must receive His grace in order to enjoy it. We must accept Christ's sacrifice for ourselves.

Never underestimate your ability as a Christ follower to usher in hope and peace, joy and life, to one who has made the weighty decision to abort a baby, or to one who is pregnant now and seriously contemplating terminating the pregnancy. As a carrier of God's grace, you may be the single flicker of light in an otherwise very dark situation. Speak with boldness. Love with gentleness. Lead with confidence. Your generosity of spirit might literally save someone's life.

to drink, or not to drink?

We drank for happiness and became unhappy.
We drank for joy and became miserable.
We drank for social ability and became argumentative.
We drank for sophistication and became obnoxious.
We drank for friendship and made enemies.
We drank for sleep and awakened without rest.
We drank for strength and felt weak.
We drank for medicinal purposes and lost our health.
We drank for relaxation and got the shakes.
We drank for bravery and became afraid.
We drank for freedom and became slaves.
We drank for confidence and become doubtful.
We drank to make our conversation easier
and it slurred our speech.
We drank to feel heavenly and ended up feeling like hell.

I f you were to add up the devastating effects of heroin, cocaine, and marijuana, it still would be less than the damage done by alcohol every day in this country. Alcohol destroys more lives, more homes, more families, and more futures, than any other drug available. And yet still we struggle to say "no." We fall prey to the massive, hundred-million-dollar marketing campaigns aimed at convincing us that "everyone drinks," and that drinking somehow will loosen us up, make us cool, bring us the life we desire. Three in four adults in the United States consume alcohol regularly, and most likely, they started young; recent studies reveal that 72 percent of high-school students have consumed alcohol, and that 37 percent of students consume it by the eighth grade.[10]

One in twelve people who begin drinking alcohol wind up addicted to it, their lives forever marked by strong drink. The Bible has a word for these folks: *unwise.*

"Wine is a mocker, strong drink a brawler," Proverbs 20:1 says, "and whoever is led astray by it is not wise."

In Proverbs 23:29-35, we read this sobering litany:

> *Who has woe? Who has sorrow? Who has strife? Who has complaining?*
> *Who has wounds without cause? Who has redness of eyes? Those who tarry long over wine; those who go to try mixed wine. Do not look at wine when it is red, when it sparkles in the cup and goes down smoothly.*

10 http://sadd.org/stats.htm

In the end it bites like a serpent and stings like an adder.
Your eyes will see strange things, and your heart utter
perverse things.
You will be like one who lies down in the midst of the sea,
like one who lies on the top of a mast.
"They struck me," you will say "but I was not hurt; they
beat me, but I did not feel it.
When shall I awake? I must have another drink."

The writer of this proverb, Solomon, isn't exactly beating
around the bush here. Forthrightly and forcefully, he offers
us a picture of what happens when alcohol leads us astray.
And it always does. It leads us astray from the wisdom we so
desperately need in this life. And if drinking alcohol leads us
away from wisdom, then it is wisdom that will lead us away
from drinking.

Frequently, when I engage someone in conversation about alcohol, and my position of abstinence begins to surface, I am greeted with a common response. "Yeah, but didn't Jesus turn water into wine?" they offer, suggesting that Jesus' first miracle, which occurred at a wedding party during which the guests had run out of wine, was an outright endorsement of imbibing whenever we please.

I always caution them about jumping to conclusions here by asking them, "Yes, but what kind of wine was it?"

Was it fermented or unfermented? The Greek word used in the Bible during that miracle is *oinos*, which could either mean something akin to grape juice, or else it could mean "strong drink." Personally, I struggle to believe that Jesus Christ would be in the liquor business. I struggle to believe He would serve up something to those wedding guests that would impair their faculties and possibly cause them harm. We are told throughout Scripture to always pursue wisdom, and to never be led astray. I believe Jesus encouraged these behaviors, even at the wedding that day.

Certainly, there are legitimate uses for alcohol noted in the Bible. In 1 Timothy 5:23, Paul told an ailing Timothy to ingest a portion of wine to help ease his stomach problems. They didn't have Pepto Bismol back then; a little wine served as a laxative that could help the digestive system heal. Proverbs 31:6 refers to alcohol as a sedative or pain reliever; "Give strong drink to the one who is perishing," it says, "and wine to those in bitter distress." In the parable of the Good Samaritan, the man who was broken and bruised and bleeding by the side of the road was greeted by a compassionate man who ministered to him by pouring oil and wine on his wounds, serving as an antiseptic solution for him.

But aside from alcohol's medicinal properties, what good does it bring to life? Let me lay out a few categories of consequence I have seen firsthand from alcohol's use.

Emotional Consequences

Alcohol causes sorrow and grief, as the proverb we looked at earlier says. It causes conflict and contention, aggressiveness and anger and corruption of every kind. It causes red eyes, strange sights, perverse thoughts, and more. It can lead to mental complications, as evidenced by more than 25 percent of patients in psychiatric wards, who are there at least in part because of alcohol's evil effects.

Alcohol can lead to depression, anxiety, self-destruction, self-loathing, and a whole host of emotional issues that short-circuit otherwise healthy lives.

Physical Consequences

Alcohol exacts a tremendous physical price as well. The consumption of alcohol has created the largest health problem in the United States when measured in terms of morbidity, and it remains the fourth largest cause of death, after heart disease, cancer, and stroke. Alcohol reduces life expectancy by a full ten years; it is to blame for half of all homicides, half of all fires, half of all drowning incidents, and a third of all suicides. Ninety-three percent of all hit-and-run accidents, 80 percent of all crime, 50 percent of all traffic fatalities, and 50 percent of all airplane crashes are linked directly to alcohol use just before the time of the tragedy.

It tastes great and is less filling, advertisers clamor for us to believe. "Taste hate; more killing" would be a more accurate slogan, perhaps.

I saw what alcohol consumption did to my dad and made a pledge as a young kid never to touch the stuff. As a pastor for nearly 40 years, I can tell you that the negative effects of alcohol on the family unit surpass *every other ill*. People drink to have a "good time," but abundance is never found in a glass. There is *no* substitute for the life-giving joy found in Christ, and Christ alone.

As a pastor for nearly 40 years, I can tell you that the negative effects of alcohol on the family unit surpass *every other ill*.

Spiritual Consequences

Spiritually, there are dire consequences as well. As parents, we will either teach our children not to drink by our mere words or by the strength of our actions. We think we can teach them to "drink responsibly," to drink moderately and not fall into addiction or pain, but even moderate habitual drinkers are killing brain cells every day.

We look at that one-in-twelve statistic I presented earlier in this chapter, thinking, "*I'll* never be the 'one' who gets addicted," but what if your (social, moderate, under-control) drinking leads to drinking by someone you love, who *does* wind up addicted? "It's not good to eat meat or drink wine or do *anything* that causes your brother to stumble," Romans 14:21 says (emphasis added). For me, it's just not worth the risk.

I teach total abstinence, because I've seen the horror show alcohol makes of a person's testimony, of his legacy, of his life. Eighty-two percent of teens will drink if their parents drink, but 72 percent will say "no" if their parents abstain. I'm asking you to make the loving choice for your family. For your friends. For your church. For those who don't yet know Jesus Christ. This isn't about hamstringing you with a bunch of legalistic rules and restrictions; it's about following biblical principles that help us *succeed*, not fail.

Whether we eat or drink, 1 Corinthians 10:31 encourages, we are to do *all things* to the glory of God. And I guess my question for you is this: can you honestly say that alcohol use and/or abuse will somehow glorify God?

> we are to do
> all things to the
> glory of God.

I've had to ask the same question of myself along the way, and my answer always is no. Think about it: what if I were to say, "Hey, I'm going to start drinking, but I'm a guy who can handle his liquor. I promise, I won't get drunk. Sure, you're going to see me bellied up to a bar now and then, but trust me, it's no big deal." How would you feel about placing your impressionable teenagers in my care? How would you feel about your friends living far from God getting their example of Christian commitment and faith from me?

I look into the eyes of countless young men and women in our church week in and week out and come away resolved in my stance that alcohol will not touch my lips. I think of them saying, "Well, if Jack Graham can handle it, then so can I," and I absolutely cringe. I hope I never fall into such self-centeredness to treat flippantly what is devouring millions day by day.

You can tell me to mind my own business on this subject, but I'll tell you that if you consume a drink and that minimal amount of alcohol delays your reflexes by two seconds, causing you to career into the car carrying one of my children or grandchildren, it most certainly becomes my business then. Please choose carefully how you will live. And I will do the same.

Yes, alcohol is dangerous. Yes, it is destructive. Yes, it addictive. Yes, it is mean. But Jesus stands ready to heal us of all its ills. Most people I share this news with stare at me with eyes that say, "I want to stop drinking, but I'm not sure I'm ready to give up what I'll have to give up." They are still living under the illusion that alcohol is filling a void in their lives that only Jesus himself can fill. I remind them of two verses that tell us otherwise: Proverbs 10:22 says that "the blessing of the Lord makes rich, and he adds *no sorrow* with it" (emphasis added), which means that when we walk in God's ways, though circumstances may disappoint us or threaten to destroy us, our hearts always can be at peace.

Then, in Psalm 84:11, we find promises that the Lord God is a "sun and shield," that He "bestows favor and honor," and that He will not withhold any "good thing from those who walk uprightly." Which begs the question related to our subject matter: What "good thing" are you looking to wine or beer or scotch to provide? May we be reminded that all *truly* good things come from our Lord, and from His hand, alone.

Give Jesus your every thought, every attitude, every action, every reaction, and yes, every habit, and watch how He transforms your life to be a closer reflection of Him.

—o○o—

5

every man's battle, and how to win

It has been my experience through four decades in pastoral ministry that every church is only as strong as its men—as strong as their faith, their ingenuity, their confidence, their resolve, their commitment to walking in the ways and will of God. I praise God for dynamic women in our churches, in our families, in our businesses, and in our homes, but there is a marvelous effect in any community when its men, specifically, are leading well.

It has also been my experience that no man can lead well who is not practicing sexual purity in his life.

Temptation is every man's battle, and every woman's as well. We all face temptations of pride and greed and rebellion, of unbelief and unkindness and unfaithfulness in our lives. But most men I have met throughout my life would readily admit that the number one temptation they face, day in and day out, centers on remaining sexually pure. We're bombarded with TV ads, magazine ads, movies that leave too little to the imagination, Internet sites that find us, regardless of how strong our filters are, and what we're left with is an overly sexualized culture, just looking to take us down.

Certainly, this isn't a new problem. We read of ancient men—prophets and kings, military leaders and shepherds, all who had wandering eyes. But I like to think our challenge is still greater today, with technology enabling instant access to smut. It's in our face 24/7, and if we're not careful, we'll dumb down our spiritual life, settling for *far* less than holiness requires.

Second Corinthians 6 holds the key, I think, to living as men of honor, men who seek hard after God. "Do not be unequally yoked with unbelievers," it says. "For what partnership has righteousness with lawlessness? Or what fellowship has light with darkness? What accord has Christ with Belial? Or what portion does a believer share with an unbeliever? What agreement has the temple of God with idols? For we are the temple of the living God; as God said, 'I will make my dwelling among them and walk among them, and I will be their God, and they shall be my people. Therefore go out from their midst, and be separate from them, says the Lord, and touch no unclean thing; then I will welcome you, and I will be a father to you, and you shall be sons and daughters to me,' says the Lord Almighty" (vv. 14-18).

The first verse of the next chapter then says: "Therefore, having these promises, beloved, let us cleanse ourselves from all filthiness of the flesh and spirit, perfecting holiness in the fear of God" (2 Corinthians 7:1).

We're not to mingle lawlessness with righteousness, darkness with light, idols with the temple of God, which according to the New Testament is our bodies—marrow and bone. Instead, we are to perfect holiness in the fear of God. What a great life goal to have!

Now, to how we accomplish that goal.

> We're not to mingle lawlessne with righteousne darkness with light, idols with t temple of God..

Prepare for Spiritual Attack

I carry around a little acronym in my mind and heart, each time I face that overly sexualized culture I mentioned earlier. The acronym is PURE, and the "P" represents "preparing for spiritual attack."

No one—including me—is above sexual temptation. First Corinthians 10:12 reminds you and me both that we who take a stand should "take heed, lest we fall." We can think that we're so steady we'll never lose our footing or trip, but King David probably thought the very same thing. And his story is a reminder to *every* man that any of us can be attacked. We have a very real enemy of our souls, who seeks to devour us as a hungry lion who has found his prey.

But the good news is this: when we arm ourselves consistently—day by day, hour by hour, moment by moment—with the presence and power of God, we become victors, not victims, over sin.

> 'e have a very real nemy of our souls, who seeks to devour us s a hungry lion who as found his prey.

Be vigilant. Stay sober-minded. Prepare for this battle in your life. And trust your loving Father to help you flee temptation's grip.

Undo Defiling Associations

The "U" in PURE represents "undoing defiling associations." This one takes raw honesty, I'll admit, because for any man who has negotiated his sexual purity by giving into temptation from time to time, admitting those failures feels like a fate worse than death. Confessing impurity is a special kind of awful, but the resulting freedom is second to none.

So, even if your wife, your children, your colleagues at work think you are morally upright, if you are falling prey to sexual temptation, you simply must find a confidant with whom you can candidly confess. You must own up to your failure so that *freedom can be yours*. First John 1:9 gives assurance that this is exactly what will take place: "If we confess our sins," it says, "he is faithful and just to forgive us our sins and to cleanse us from all unrighteousness." Cleansing from all unrighteousness—isn't this what we truly desire?

Then, going forward, rid yourself of any and all "defiling associations." If there are people or places that promote temptation in your mind and heart, *get them out of your life*. Sever the ties. Bid fond farewells. Save yourself from agonizing harm. This may mean adding filters to your Internet, discontinuing all private communication with

> If there are people
> places that promo
> temptation in your
> mind and heart, *ge*
> *them out of your lif*

certain work associates, making sure your spouse is present whenever you visit certain neighbors, avoiding situations in coffee shops or restaurants or hotels or business meetings that you *know* only lead you astray.

For more than thirty-five years, I have made it a practice never to go to lunch (or breakfast or dinner, for that matter) with a woman other than my wife, unless my wife also is present. I don't travel alone with another woman, even if that means a simple, cross-town car ride. And this isn't merely for the sake of appearances, although that is also a worthwhile goal. It is for the sake of my soul. It is to help me remain sexually pure.

Rarely does a week go by when a man doesn't request a meeting with me to discuss his moral failure. Maybe it centered on indulging in online pornography. Maybe he had begun placing too high a value on compliments from his assistant at work. Maybe it was that he actually met that assistant at a local hotel at 2 a.m., while his family was visiting his in-laws two states away. What he once prized as his "secret sin" now was consuming every aspect of his life. As the old saying goes, we don't keep secrets, as much as our secrets keep us.

—o-o-o—

We must rid our lives of the associations that are keeping us in bondage, in sin, and in pain.

Remember the Consequences of Fatal Attractions

A movie came out in the late 1980s that set men's feet on the straight-and-narrow path better than any good sermon ever could. Dan Gallagher—played by Michael Douglas—was a successful and happily married attorney living in New York who had what he considered "an innocent weekend fling" with a female business associate turn very, very bad. The "other woman" refused to cut ties with Dan and wound up terrorizing his entire family as a result. In the end, the attraction did prove fatal, as Dan's wife shot his mistress in the chest. But perhaps equally devastating to the philandering husband was having to repair the breach of trust he'd caused with his wife, his daughter, and himself.

We do well to remember the consequences of fatal attractions—the "R" in our PURE acronym—which often include a broken marriage, the loss of loved ones' respect, the loss of employment, exposure to disease, the destruction of our witness and testimony for Christ, the loss of leadership in the church … the list can go on. Sexual sin seems enticing on the surface, but there is a monster lurking underneath. The Bible refers to that monster by name: Sin Against Your Own Soul. This particular sin—the sin of sexual immorality—wages war in your mind, in your body, in your relationships, in your Christian witness, and yes, even in your soul. Which is why the aftereffects can be so terribly tough to move through. But again, this is where Jesus paves the way, beckoning us onward and upward toward that perfected holiness we seek.

Engage in Positive Spiritual Activities

There is a fourth letter in our PURE acronym—"E"—which stands for *engaging in positive spiritual activities*. You and I never will win the battle against sexual temptation simply by telling ourselves "no": No to this, no to that, no to this, no to that. In addition, we must say some appropriate yeses: yes to holiness, yes to cleanliness, yes to righteousness, yes to faithfulness, yes to God's presence and power and peace.

> e can say yes,
> r example, to
> rtifying our faith,
> ⱽ writing God's
> ord on our hearts.

We can say yes, for example, to fortifying our faith, by writing God's Word on our hearts. For starters, I recommend memorizing Psalm 119:11: "I have stored up your word in my heart, that I might not sin against you." Next, as that verse says, go ahead and start "storing up" in your heart other gems from the living, active Word of God. 2 Timothy 2:22 might encourage you: "So flee youthful passions and pursue righteousness, faith, love, and peace, along with those who call on the Lord from a pure heart." Or how about Psalm 51:9-11, for those times when you've failed but long to get back on God's path? It reads:

Hide your face from my sins, and blot out my iniquities.
Create in me a clean heart, O God, and renew a right spirit
within me.
Cast me not away from your presence,
and take not your Holy Spirit from me.

We can also say yes to purifying our thoughts. Philippians 4:8 reminds us that we have control over what we think about, and that we can choose helpful, healthy thoughts. "Whatever things are true, whatever things are noble, whatever things are just, whatever things are pure, whatever things are lovely, whatever things are of good report," it reads, "if there is any virtue and if there's anything praiseworthy, meditate on these things." To purify our thoughts, we must *meditate*, the verse says, on things that honor God.

We can say yes to having an accountability partner. As I mentioned earlier, if you are struggling with sexual sin, find someone more mature in the faith who can listen to your confessions and encourage you along healing's path.

> when you fully devote yourself to living for Jesus every day, you'll find He gladly mops up your life's messes...

And finally, we can say yes to magnifying the Lord Jesus in our lives. What countless millions of Christ followers have discovered—and what you certainly will discover, too—is that when you fully devote yourself to living for Jesus every day, you'll find He gladly mops up your life's messes, left and right. He'll clean up your mind, your heart, your attitude, your actions, your desires, your cravings, your habits, and your sin. In fact, over time, you'll notice that your love for that sin is being replaced by an insatiable love for *Christ*. Your prayers will deepen, as you genuinely long to sit in His presence and learn more of who He is. You'll tell Him earnestly, "I really don't want any part of something that will compromise my intimacy with you." You'll find purity taking hold of you, where sin once had full reign.

Ephesians 5:3-5 raises the bar on our activity as people of God: "But among you there must not be even a *hint* of sexual immorality, or of any kind of impurity, or of greed, because these are improper for God's holy people. Nor should there be obscenity, foolish talk or coarse joking, which are out of place, but rather thanksgiving. For of this you can be sure: No immoral, impure or greedy person—such as person is an idolater—has any inheritance in the kingdom of Christ and of God" (NIV, emphasis added).

Not even a *hint* of sexual sin, it says! This is why we need the power of Christ working in our lives, right? Not. Even. A. Hint.

May perfected holiness have its way in our lives.

Author Randy Alcorn once described sexual sin in terms that have stuck with me ever since: "A battering ram may hit a fortress gate a thousand times and no one time seems to have an effect; yet finally the gate caves in. Likewise, immorality is the cumulative product of small mental indulgences and miniscule promises or compromises, the immediate consequences of which are, at the time, indiscernible. One thought is the fabric of which we weave our character and our destiny."

Let's be wise stewards of each thought we indulge, each decision we make, each action we take, so that we don't run the risk of our lives' gates caving in.

are same-sex relationships really the same?

Recently I came across a popular weekly news magazine boasting the cover story, "What's Next for the Gay Agenda." The implication here, of course, is that there is an agenda, as it relates to promoting same-sex relationships in this country, and that the agenda is moving forward, even as I type. Increasingly, homosexuality is being viewed as an acceptable—in many cases, even *desirable*—lifestyle.

As recently as 1960, every state in the Union had an anti-sodomy law, but as of 2003, when the Supreme Court struck down such laws in the remaining fourteen states that had them, the doors were swung wide open to a revolution in the definition and practice of "family," which would produce shifts in marital status, government benefits, adoptions practices, and more. Justice Antonin Scalia, one of the dissenting judges in the case to ban the final sodomy laws said, "The Supreme Court has now taken sides in the cultural war. The Court has largely signed on to the so-called homosexual agenda. This will result in a massive disruption of the social order."[11]

The message from that 2003 ruling was hard to miss: you cannot legislate morality. Which makes the church's task clearer-cut still: we must speak up for righteousness, for God's desired plan for how His people will live. My goal is not to condemn people who wrestle with sexual-orientation issues; rather, I want to expose us to what God's Word has to say on the subject and compel us to seek His wisdom for how we should then respond. This subject of same-sex relationship has moved from the margins to the mainstream of our society and is not going away any time soon. As lovers of God and followers of Christ, we must educate ourselves so that in all grace, humility, and compassion, we can respond with thoughtful *truth*.

> As lovers of God and followers of Christ, we must educate ourselves so that in all grace, humility, and compassion, we can respond with thoughtful *truth*.

The Bible's View on Homosexuality

Even a cursory reading of Scripture proves to us that the practice of homosexuality is almost as old as man; in chapters 18 and 19 of Genesis, we read of Sodom and Gomorrah,

[11] "Supreme Court Strikes Down Texas Law Banning Sodomy," The Associated Press, 26 June 2003.

two kingdoms that God chose to destroy because of their persistent immorality and perversion. As the story goes, two angels and God himself paid a visit to Abraham, God's chosen man to be the "father of many nations." God told Abraham that the outcry against Sodom and Gomorrah was so great—and their sin so terribly grievous—that He simply must take action against them. In response, Abraham pleaded with God to have mercy on the cities, specifically because his nephew, Lot, and Lot's family were living in Sodom at the time. He couldn't bear to see his nephew harmed.

Abraham and God then undertook a negotiation, with God eventually promising that if He could find even *ten* righteous people in the city of Sodom, He would spare the entire population.

The angels of the Lord then proceeded to Sodom, disguised as human men, and were met by Lot in the city square, who urged them to stay at his home. The angels agreed, but by nightfall, the house where they were staying was utterly surrounded by the city's men. And things were not looking good. The men of the city shouted to Lot, "Where are the men who came to you tonight? Bring them out to us, that we may know them." In plain terms, this was a homosexual gang rape waiting to happen. And God, understandably, was not pleased.

The angels blinded the men of the city, they begged Lot to flee with his family, and they stood back as God rained down burning sulfur on the cities, destroying everything in plain sight.

So what, exactly, was their sin?

Ezekiel 16:49-50 says, "Behold, this was the guilt of your sister Sodom: she and her daughters had pride, excess of food, and prosperous ease, but did not aid the poor and needy. They were haughty and did an abomination before me. So I removed them, when I saw it."

Certainly, Sodom—and neighboring Gomorrah—were guilty of a slew of horrendous sins. But it is undeniable that homosexuality—the "abomination" referenced in Ezekiel— played a pivotal role in God destroying them and all their inhabitants, and why still today the area where the cities once stood remains a deserted wasteland.

The Bible is clear about God's posture toward homosexuality: not once does it endorse same-sex attraction or activity. Not *once*. In

The Bible is clear about God's posture toward homosexuality: not once does it endorse same-sex attraction or activity.

the Old Testament and the New Testament alike, we find patriarchs, prophets, and apostles who never once lowered their standards of sexuality to accommodate the sexual immorality of their times. In fact, the Bible strictly *forbids* such behavior.

In Romans 1:26-27, the apostle Paul says that because people were turning the worship of the one, true God into corruption and idol worship, God "gave them up to vile passions. For even their women exchanged the natural use for what is against nature. Likewise, also the men leaving the natural use of the woman, burned in their lust for one another, men with men committing what is shameful and receiving in themselves the penalty of their error which was due."

When we choose to rebel against God in our sexual lives, God chooses to give us what it is we say we crave, even if it is a perversion of His will and ways. There is no such thing as "natural homosexuality"; it is *always* the result of deviance in our lives, and the Bible prohibits it as vehemently as it prohibits adultery and fornication and all other such acts. It is commonplace for those involved in a same-sex relationship to say, "I've always been this way. I've never been attracted to the opposite sex ..." but science remains astoundingly unclear on whether it is by nature or by nurture that a person leans toward homosexuality. There is simply no conclusive evidence to support the idea that people are helplessly at the mercy of a same-sex attraction.

> There is simply no conclusive evidence to support the idea that people are helplessly at the mercy of a same-sex attraction.

Since the beginning of time, God's intention has been that one man and one woman would join together, forsaking all others and leaving their families of origin to form a new union, a new family all their own. There was no gender confusion when God established man on the earth. "So God created man in his own image, in the image of God he created him," says Genesis 1:27; "*male and female* he created them" (emphasis added).

Before any other institution existed, political or religious or otherwise, God established the institution of family—one man, one woman, and the ability and desire to produce heirs.

Marriage is for One Man and One Woman

So, the first God-given purpose for the marital union is to bring together one man and one woman in a covenantal way. Marriage is the building block of humanity, the original framework by which men and women experience intimacy and productivity. Men are to protect and provide for and love their women; women are to support, serve, and sacrifice for their men. Both are to balance the other one out, to contribute physically, socially, psychologically, and spiritually to the other one's life.

The late Chuck Colson once astutely observed that "the argument we see is that to deny homosexuals marriage is manifestly unfair. But it is not unfair. Gays and lesbians are not unworthy of marriage; they are *incapable* of marriage." According to Scripture, Colson is absolutely correct. Man's sexual identity is defined by God, not by man. Marriage is defined by God, not by man. Marriage is for *one woman and one man*, and only one woman and one man.

> Marriage is define by God, not by man. Marriage is for *one woman and one man*, ar only one woman and one man.

Marriage is for Producing and Providing for Children

The second purpose of marriage is to produce and provide for children. Marriage ensures that children have the benefits of growing up with both a father and a mother—the masculine and the feminine—a framework evidently extremely important to God. This is God's best for the crown of His creation, His people. It is His ordained and optimal plan.

The Implications of Going Against God

From a practical standpoint, the implications of choosing sinfulness as a lifestyle are severe. Same-sex relationships differ from those involving one man and one woman in at least six troubling ways:

- Relationship duration
- Level of promiscuity—in one study I came across, it was reported that the average gay male in America has more than 100 sexual partners in his lifetime
- Level of relational commitment
- Number of children
- Health risks
- Rate of intimate-partner violence

More troubling still is God's take on the matter. Little is left to the imagination regarding what will happen to those who insist on rebelling against God in a consistent and conscious manner: "Do you not know that the unrighteous will not inherit the kingdom of God?" asks 1 Corinthians 6:9. "Do not be deceived; neither fornicators, nor idolaters, nor adulterers, nor homosexuals, nor sodomites, nor thieves, nor covetousness, nor drunkards, nor revilers, nor extortioners will inherit the kingdom of God."

If we insist on practicing a lifestyle inclusive of these sins, we will not be part of the kingdom of God. This ought to drive us to our knees every day, on behalf of every person we know suffering in sin.

How God's People Can be Salt and Light

First Corinthians 6:11 reminds us that regardless of how morally we try to live, none of us is without sin. Immediately on the heels of the litany of sins that will keep people from inheriting the kingdom of God, Paul looks into the eyes of members of the admittedly lascivious culture who were seated before him and said, "and such were some of you." He could have delivered the very same sentiment before any church in North America today: "And such were some of you." Such were some of

> First Corinthians 6:11 reminds us that regardless of how morally we t to live, none of us is without sin.

us. Such were you and me both: we know what it is to walk in rebellion against God, don't we? *All* have sinned and fall short of the glory of God (Romans 3:23).

But the verse doesn't end there. "But you were *washed*," it says, "you were *sanctified*, you were *justified* in the name of the Lord Jesus and by the Spirit of God" (emphasis added). The same can be true for *anyone* walking in any form of sin today. The God who has set the feet of countless thousands of people involved in same-sex relationships on the path of His will and ways stands ready to deliver them all. As a church, we are called to help restoration run its course.

Promote Deliverance, Not Tolerance

As Christ's followers, we can first promote deliverance, rather than tolerance. We can proclaim boldly the message that people can be delivered, saved, and transformed into new creations by the perfecting power of God. If a person is willing to repent and trust Christ with his or her life, that person immediately is healed of sin's reign over his or her heart. It's not to say their leanings or attractions *immediately* disappear. Or that repercussions from past decisions won't linger on into future days. But spiritually speaking, their standing before Christ is upright.

We are not called to show anything but kindness and helpfulness, grace and compassion to the person trapped in homosexuality, even as we speak the truth of God's Word. We loathe the sin; we love the sinner—this distinction simply must be made.

Protect the Institution of the Family

Secondly, we can do everything possible to protect God's design for the family. The best way to defeat the gay agenda is to follow the pattern for biblical family in your own home, and to ensure that you are living according to the principles of God's Word. We must not condemn in others what we refuse to practice ourselves. We must model for our children God's ideal structure for men and women and children; we must talk to our kids about issues of sexuality and deviance, and the implications for rebelling against God; we must balance what our kids are learning in the classroom and on the playground with unchanging biblical truth; and we must ask God for wisdom at every turn, as we educate friends, neighbors, and work colleagues about His desire for *every* woman, *every* man.

We are not called to show anything but kindness and helpfulness, grace and compassion to the person trapped in homosexuality...

—◦◦◦—

Practice Christian Citizenship

third thing we can do to fight for God's ways in the realm of sexuality is to practice Christian citizenship by expressing our voice through our vote.

A third thing we can do to fight for God's ways in the realm of sexuality is to practice Christian citizenship by expressing our voice through our vote. Collectively we may be a voice crying in the wilderness, but that voice can be prophetic instead of pathetic! Stay informed. Prepare reasonable responses to the arguments that matter. Engage in the debate. And connect through letters, e-mails, and in-person meetings with representatives tasked with making legislative decisions affecting our homes, our schools, our cities, our nation, and our world at large.

Pray for Those in Bondage to Sexual Sin

Finally, to live as Christ's follower at that magnificent intersection of conviction and compassion, commit yourself to praying for those who are stuck in bondage to sexual sin. The power of prayer really can change lives. Pray for their eyes to be opened to their sinfulness. Pray for their hearts to be receptive to the work of the Holy Spirit. Pray for the chains of bondage to be broken in their lives. Pray for their restoration, for their renewal, for their re-establishment as inheritors of the kingdom of God.

In his book *Homosexuality: Disease or Way of Life?*, Dr. Edmund Bergler writes, "The homosexual's real enemy is … his ignorance of the possibility that he can be helped."[12] May we be conduits of God's presence, His power, and His very real desire to help *everyone* who wishes to be helped.

[12] Dr. Edmund Bergler, Homosexuality: Disease or Way of Life? (New York: Collier Books, 1962), p. 227.

7

money, money, money

> "I'm working as hard as I can to get my life and my cash to run out at the same time. And if I die right after lunch on Tuesday, everything will be fine."
>
> —former pro golfer Doug Sanders

A fascinating story appears in the book of Nehemiah about one man who led an entire nation to accomplish a lofty goal. Nehemiah was serving as cupbearer to the king, far away from his homeland of Judah, when he was visited by some of his old Jewish friends. He asked about the state of affairs in Judah—was everyone okay, following the exile? How was the city of Jerusalem holding up?

The answers troubled him deeply. Famine had struck, the region was in ruins, the city's protective walls were in a state of disrepair. The people were hopeless, hapless, and in desperate need of help, and Nehemiah knew he was the man for the job. And so, he fasted. He prayed. He begged his heavenly Father to have mercy on his people, and to allow Nehemiah to be released from his duties with the king long enough to help rebuild Jerusalem's walls.

Favor was with Nehemiah, and not only did the king approve Nehemiah's departure, but also he provided resources to make his trip quick and smooth. Nehemiah arrived in town, he rallied a group of fellow wall-builders around him, and he assured his posse that God was on their side—that the wall would *definitely* get rebuilt.

In the end, Nehemiah would be right about that: the wall did, in fact, get rebuilt. But not without opposition that Nehemiah never knew to predict.

Along the way, there were mockers who hurled insults at Nehemiah and his team, almost daring them to succeed. There were fellow Jews whose resentment, cynicism, and ridicule made it difficult to keep at the job. There were those with ill intent, who imperiled the team's very lives. Through all of these challenges, Nehemiah encouraged his team to focus not on their enemy, but on the Lord, who stood by their side. "Our God will fight for us!" (Nehemiah 4:20, MSG) Nehemiah promised his ranks. They simply could not afford to give up.

But then, Satan's intended coup de grâce: when he couldn't thwart Nehemiah's team's efforts with discouragement, defeatism, or outright danger to their lives, he decided to employ a sure-fire tool from his evil arsenal, a tool that has been debilitating believers since the beginning of time: *financial bondage.* Nehemiah 5:1-5 says:

> *Now there arose a great outcry of the people and of their wives against their Jewish brothers. For there were those who said, "With our sons and our daughters, we are many. So let us get grain, that we may eat and keep alive." There were also those who said, "We are mortgaging our fields, our vineyards, and our houses to get grain because of the famine." And there were those who said, "We have borrowed money for the king's tax on our fields and our vineyards. Now our flesh is as the flesh of our brothers, our children are as their children. Yet we are forcing our sons and our daughters to be slaves, and some of our daughters have already been enslaved, but it is not in our power to help it, for other men have our fields and our vineyards."*

Nehemiah's people had fallen into a pit of financial failure, and they saw absolutely no way out.

Misuse of Money Causes Conflict

The children of Israel were living in bondage financially, which was causing turmoil in their hearts individually, and also turmoil in their dealings with each other. Which is typical, isn't it? You and I both can relate to the conflict money-problems cause. We see conflict in our government, we see conflict in our country's businesses, we see conflict in our churches, we see conflict in our families—and it all hinges on the almighty buck. It is said that more than 56 percent of divorces stem from conflict over money, money, money. Indeed, a house divided cannot stand, especially when the dissention deals with cash.

Former Senate Chaplain Richard Halverson once summed up the crucial role management of money plays in our lives: "Jesus Christ said more about money than any other single thing, because money is of the first importance when it comes to a man's real nature. Money is an exact index to a man's true character. All through Scripture there is an intimate correlation between the development of a man's character and how he handles money."

It is said that mor than 56 percent of divorces stem from conflict over money, money, money.

Chaplain Halverson has it right: how we handle money speaks volumes about whether we are greedy or generous, selfish or selfless, consumer-minded or consecrated to God. The Israelites were overextended in their money life. They were leveraging their houses to buy food, proving financial bondage was running its course. And slavery is never fun.

A generation or two ago, when our grandparents and great-grandparents didn't have enough money to buy something, they practiced the novel idea of *not buying it*. But with today's proliferation of credit cards beckoning us to simply "charge it," the majority of people in this country get sucked in and max out fast.

> A generation or two ago, when our grandparents and great-grandparents didn't have enough money to buy something, they practiced the novel idea of *not buying it*.

Of the nearly 200 million Americans who have credit cards, their average total household debt is just more than $15,900[13]. Nearly sixteen thousand dollars owed, on plastic "gimme now" cards! And with interest rates on those cards sometimes cresting 20 percent, it's no wonder people have likened the process of getting out of debt to climbing an icy mountain.

[13] http://www.creditcards.com/credit-card-news/credit-card-industry-facts-personal-debt-statistics-1276.php

When I meet with people who fear they, too, may be enslaving themselves financially, I ask them to run through a top-ten list of indicators that quickly assesses their "bondage quotient." See how you fare, as you review the following points:

1. Are you charging daily expenditures—necessities of daily living—to credit cards, because you have a lack of funds?

2. Are you procrastinating paying a bill until "next month"?

3. Are you borrowing money in order to pay fixed expenses such as a mortgage payment, an insurance payment, or your electric bill?

4. Are you unaware of how much you really owe your creditors?

5. Do you have creditors call on you or write to you, to alert you to past-due bills?

6. Are you taking money from your savings account, to pay regular, monthly bills?

7. Are you taking out new loans in order to pay off the old ones?

8. Do you and your loved ones argue over money?

9. Do you consider being dishonest, unscrupulous, or

unethical—even "just once"—in order to help make this month's ends meet?

10. Do you find it difficult to return God's tithe to God's house on God's day each week?

If you answered "yes" to any of the above items, you are in some level of financial bondage. And this type of bondage will affect every aspect of your life. It will keep you up at night. It will fracture your marriage. It will hamstring your relationship with your children. It will preoccupy you at work. It will cause ailments in your physical body, not to mention exceptionally high levels of stress. It will keep you from investing, saving, and giving from the overflow of your heart. It will make you irritable and defensive and sad.

> . financial bondage vill keep you from ving the life God has alled you to live.

But there is a *worse* effect still, which is that financial bondage will keep you from living the life God has called you to live. You will want to be part of God's divine work in the world, and yet because of your sorry financial condition, you'll have to watch from the sidelines while others who have mastered their money enjoy a fulfilling, full-throttle ride. God's desire for us is that we would live not enslaved, but rather, that by His truth, we'd be *set free.* (See John 8:32.)

Financial Stewardship Causes Peace

God promises blessing, not bondage, when we follow His will and His ways. Deuteronomy 28:2-6 lays out in plain terms the blessings that await us:

> *God's blessing inside the city,*
> *God's blessing in the country;*
> *God's blessing on your children,*
> *the crops of your land,*
> *the young of your livestock,*
> *the calves of your herds,*
> *the lambs of your flocks.*
> *God's blessing on your basket and bread bowl;*
> *God's blessing in your coming in,*
> *God's blessing in your going out.*

Don't we both crave blessings such as these?

Verse 8 continues the coveted list: "God will order a blessing on your barns and workplaces; he'll bless you in the land that

God, your God, is giving you." And then, in verses 11 and 12, we read: "God will lavish you with good things: children from your womb, offspring from your animals, and crops from your land, the land that God promised your ancestors that he would give you. God will throw open the doors of His sky vaults and pour rain on your land on schedule and bless the work you take in hand."

We read a list such as this and find ourselves salivating in eager desire: "Yes, Lord, yes! I'll take one of each, please!" But in my experience, people are far more interested in receiving the blessing than they are in honoring the two requests God makes of us first. Verse 1 of Deuteronomy 28 makes clear what we must do: "If you listen obediently to the Voice of God, your God, and heartily obey all his commandments that I command you today, God, your God, will place you on high, high above all the nations of the world. All these blessings will come down on you and spread out beyond you because you have responded to the Voice of God, your God."

If we want to live blessed instead of in bondage, we must *listen*, and we must *obey*. *Obedience* is what brings blessing. *Disobedience* is what keeps us enslaved.

> we want to live
> essed instead of
> bondage, we
> ust *listen*, and
> e must *obey*.

—o-o-o—

There is a Way Out of Debilitating Debt

We have been abundantly blessed by our loving and generous God. All we must do now is live in such a way so as to receive it. We must first listen, and then obey. What follows are three practical steps you can take, to begin to obey God in your finances.

Tell the Truth

Back to our story in Nehemiah 5. Just after Nehemiah listened to the rants and raves of his financially strapped colleagues, the text says he got very angry. But instead of lashing out impulsively, he first thought things over. "I took counsel with myself," verse 6 says, "and I brought charges against the nobles and the officials. I said to them, 'You are exacting interest, each from his brother.' "

> We have been abundantly blessed by our loving and generous God. All we must do now is live in such a way so as to receive

Nehemiah's first step toward helping free his people from financial bondage involved "taking counsel" with himself. This must be our first step, too.

If you are suffering in financial bondage today, then it's absolutely critical that you come clean with your struggle.

Stop covering up the problem, stop deceiving your friends and loved ones, stop pretending things will miraculously get better on their own. Proverbs 21:5 says that "the plans of the diligent lead surely to abundance"; in other words, we are wise when we effectively *plan*.

So, come before God and in a spirit of humility admit the reality you are facing. Tell the truth. Get upset over it. Apologize for it. And then receive His grace and forgiveness so that you can begin to make right what is wrong.

Take Decisive Action

After you tell the truth about your situation, it is then time to take decisive action. Nehemiah did just that: in verses 9 through 13, the great leader laid out a detailed plan for his people to follow, involving abandoning harmful financial practices, living within their means, and squelching the self-centeredness that had gotten them into trouble to begin with. There's a lesson here for you and me both.

Reduce your spending

To break bondage's claim on your life, first, you must reduce your spending. This probably sounds like a declaration of the obvious, but I'm always surprised by how many needless expenditures people willingly incur month to month, when they're drowning in a sea of red ink. Things such as four-dollar coffee drinks, monthly satellite-TV subscriptions, cellphone plans, and a few lunches out with friends are not inherently bad, but when you're not able to see straight because your debt level is taking you under, you might consider giving them up—at least for a time.

Ask God to help you sort out your needs from your "greeds," remembering that He has committed himself to supplying every single [true] need you have. (See Philippians 4:19.)

Budget your income.

Next, budget your income. Gather your family together and say, "Kids, we're going to live a different kind of life for a while so that we can solve the problems that we face." Write down your monthly income; subtract your tithe and fixed expense; such as mortgage payments, utility bills, and car and health insurance; and then divide what remains across your debt payments and living expenses. You may need to boost your savings or set aside monies for children's education funds, but these things must take a backseat to the pressing need to free yourself from debt.

Focus not on getting, but on giving.

Finally, focus on what you can *give* and not what you can *get*. At the end of Nehemiah 5, we read that instead of expensing the costs associated with rebuilding the walls surrounding Jerusalem, Nehemiah paid out-of-pocket for many of them and even hosted a banquet for 150 people as a simple act of generosity. He had learned to be a giver, not a taker, and God was blessing him richly as a result.

Later, in the New Testament, we read Jesus' exhortation along these same lines: "… give, and it will be given unto you. Good measure, pressed down, shaken together, and running over will be put into your lap" (Luke 6:38). This is astoundingly good advice! I dare you to try it sometime. I challenge you to stop trying to sort out how you can get more in this life—more recognition, more opportunities, more money, more power, more prestige, more advancement, more toys—and instead try to sort out how you can give, give, give more away. Sacrifice something, so that someone might come to know Christ. Bless someone somewhere, so that they may know a good God exists. Listen closely to that still, small voice that asks you, "When are you going to give something away, instead of acquiring more and more?"

Change your focus, and you'll change your life. I promise you, this much is true.

The fifth chapter of Nehemiah closes with the leader recounting his faithfulness to his God and then asking God to bless him as a result: "Remember for my good, O my God, all that I have done for this people" (Nehemiah 5:19). And based on Nehemiah's depth of relationship with the Almighty, I would venture a guess that the man knew God would *gladly* bless him, in return for obediently following God. This is how God works, remember? Obedience yields blessing. Always has, and always will.

8

capital punishment: what's love got to do with it?

Karla Faye Tucker was born and raised in Houston, Texas, the third daughter of parents enduring a very troubled marriage. By twelve years old, Karla had turned to drugs and sex to find acceptance and fulfillment—things she hadn't received at home. Her parents had divorced by then, and at age fourteen Karla decided to drop out of school and follow her mom around, who was living as a rock-band groupie and prostitute. Karla married a mechanic at age sixteen, but the union quickly fell apart. In her early twenties, Karla met a man, Danny Garrett, who also was addicted to drugs, and the two began using together.

One weekend, while in a drug-induced stupor, Tucker and Garrett entered the home of their "friend," Jerry Dean, at three in the morning, intending to steal Dean's motorcycle. Dean was awakened by the entry, and before the sun rose the next morning, he would be dead. Garrett had hit Dean's head repeatedly with such force that Dean's head had

—○-○-○—

come unhinged from his neck. Dean began gurgling as his breathing passages filled with fluid; to stop the annoying gurgling sound, Tucker attacked Dean with a pickaxe. While Tucker finished off Dean, Garrett continued making trips back and forth from the house to his car, carting off Dean's motorcycle parts and claiming them as his own.

When Dean was all but dead, Tucker then noticed a woman hiding underneath the bed covers, who had been there all along. A scuffle ensued until Tucker embedded the pickaxe in the woman's heart. Then she stabbed her again. And again. And again. Tucker later would tell a jury that she experienced intense sexual pleasure each time she wielded that axe.

In September 1983, Tucker and Garrett were indicted and tried separately for the two murders. Soon after being imprisoned, Tucker reportedly picked up a Bible from the prison's ministry program and read it while in her cell. "I didn't know what I was reading," she would say. "But before I knew it, I was down on my knees on the cold cement floor of my jail cell, giving my heart to Jesus Christ, begging God to somehow forgive me for the awful things I'd done."

Karla Faye Tucker became a Christ follower in October

—o0o—

1983, and later married prison minister Reverend Dana Lane Brown, while still incarcerated. She was executed by lethal injection in the Huntsville Unit in Huntsville, Texas, on February 3, 1998, the first woman to be executed in Texas since the Civil War. Just before she was injected, she was praising Jesus and thanking the few friends gathered there for their kindness, forgiveness, and grace.

And with her execution came outcries from both sides: "Capital punishment is legalized murder!" some claimed, while others rallied around the idea that it's essential for maintaining law and order in a just and civilized society. So, which is it? What do you say?

More importantly, what does *God* say?

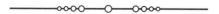

Capital punishment is as old as recorded time. In the ninth chapter of Genesis, we find God raging in anger over rampant disobedience and exterminating the entire population of people that He Himself had made. After the flood waters receded, only eight people remained—Noah, his wife, his three sons, and their wives. "Now, it's just you," God essentially told them. "Now, we will start again."

God made a covenant with Noah, that He would never again flood the earth. He delivered every beast of the field and every bird of the air into Noah's hands, to rule over, to steward, to eat. And, finally, He explained to Noah that He would demand a reckoning for every man's life to come. "Whoever sheds the blood of man, by man shall his blood be shed," God said, "for God made man in his own image" (verse 6).

And with that, the mandate had been given to mankind, to care for all human life. Human life is *precious*, God was saying. It is *sacred*. It is *holy*, because it is made in the image of God. To take the life of someone else is to defame and desecrate the image of God. It is to willfully destroy what God meticulously made.

Furthermore, in Romans 12:17-19, we read the following:

> *Repay no one evil for evil, but give thought to do*
> *what is honorable in the sight of all. If possible, so far as*

it depends on you, live peaceably with all. Beloved, never avenge yourselves, but leave it to the wrath of God, for it is written, "Vengeance is mine, I will repay, says the Lord."

Scripture is clear here: we must never repay evil for evil, meaning that when you and I are wronged, we must *refuse the temptation* to wrong the ones who wronged us. We are to give room for God to exact retribution He feels is fitting, based on the wrong that was done. It's not our job to pay people back; that job is God's, alone. We are to *bless* those who curse us, and *pray* for those who mean us harm (see Luke 6:28).

Every sin committed here on this earth either will be pardoned by Christ or punished in hell; either way, the action is God's to take. Romans 13 reveals one such way that God takes action to punish sin. Verses 1 through 4 say: "Let every person be subject to the governing authorities. For there is no authority except from God, and those that exist have been instituted by God. Therefore whoever resists the authorities resists what God has appointed, and those who resist will incur judgment. For rulers are not a terror to good conduct, but to bad. Would you have no fear of the one who is in authority? Then do what is good, and you will receive his approval, for he is God's servant for your good. But if you do wrong, be afraid, for he does not bear the sword in vain. For he is the servant of God, an avenger who carries out God's wrath on the wrongdoer."

One of the ways God exacts punishment for wrongdoing is through governing authorities, those who "bear the sword," whom God *Himself* has placed in power. God is righteous. He is holy. He is blameless and perfect and just. Sin *angers* him. Sin *distances* him. Sin must face punishment of some kind. And God authorizes human leaders to help Him accomplish this task—"servants," He calls them in the verses we just read—who help God carry out His wrath against wrongdoing. Police officers, mayors, judges, magistrates—these and many other roles have been directly ordained by God.

Remember the scene when Jesus was standing before Pilate, receiving judgment from the earthly king? Jesus looked at him and said, "You have no power, no authority, except that which has been given to you from above." *All* power is given by God, who holds *all* power in His hands.

All powe[r] is given [by] God, wh[o] holds all power i[n] His hanc[s]

To recap: Since the dawn of time, capital punishment has been one means of God dealing with injustice and wrongdoing in the earth. He explicitly states that this is a tool in *His* hands, though, not in ours. Now, with that as a backdrop, let's look at four considerations regarding the complex issues surrounding capital punishment.

> es, God's love is
> trong and powerful
> nd everlasting. But
> is not sentimental.

The Love of God

The first consideration regarding capital punishment is that *God is love*. Sometimes I say this to folks who are decidedly anti-capital punishment, and I get a perplexed look in response. "Huh? God is *love*? What could that possibly have to do with *this* debate?"

It actually plays a critical role.

To those who wonder how a good and kind God could allow something as obviously *not good* and *unkind* as capital punishment—and typically, these are the same people who wonder how a good and kind God could allow something as not good and unkind as hell—I remind them that it is in fact God's *goodness*—His *kindness*—that leads to repentance. Yes, God's love is strong and powerful and everlasting. But it is not sentimental. It is not shallow. It demands something in return.

When you and I truly apprehend the love of God, we simultaneously abhor what is unlovely, the evils of this world. "Let love be sincere," the apostle Paul once said (see Romans 12:9), meaning, "Let love be pure, and faithful, and clinging to all that is good."

It is because of God's love that He simply must punish sin. He cannot share space with sin; He can't look upon it and remain holy, and we know from Scripture that His holiness *always* remains. Because He prizes people—the "crown of creation," we're called in His Word—He works to protect us from unrestrained evil. He works to execute judgment of the sin that so easily traps us and entangles us and threatens to do us in.

This judgment knows no race, no background, no socioeconomic status, and no religion, as Karla Faye Tucker's

> God must puni.
> *sin*, regardless o
> who the sinner

case proved. God must punish *sin*, regardless of who the sinner is. And sometimes He does it through capital punishment. Sometimes, this is what He demands.

The Welfare of Society

A second consideration in the debate regarding whether we as a society ought to pursue capital punishment as a form of serving justice is the welfare of that society in question. Indeed, our society is sick, and whenever you're sick, the goal is the eradication of the agent causing the illness. It is not cruel or unusual, for instance, for a doctor to remove cancerous tumors from an otherwise healthy body. Similarly, when a member of our society forfeits his or her right to live as a free individual, it is not cruel or unusual to remove that person from our midst. Certainly, those who continue to live freely ought to make it part of their ongoing mission in life to pray for and visit incarcerated people, to share God's message of grace with them, to work to see them fully restored emotionally, psychologically, and spiritually. But when they are unable to be restored *physically* to free society, we must understand that capital punishment is not outside the bounds of God's original design for eradicating evil from this world.

When in discussions with people on this highly controversial topic, I've often heard that a primary reason they are against capital punishment is that studies show the practice of executing criminals does nothing to deter future crime. I always beg to differ, for two reasons. One is theoretical, the other practical. In theory, if we say that we should discontinue capital punishment because it does not deter crime, we must we willing to say that we should discontinue *all* forms of punishment, on the basis that wrongdoing still occurs, even in light of the potential for traffic tickets that exact monetary fines, probation, or incarceration.

Of course, this is foolishness. Human beings' recklessness regarding crime's consequences must not cause us as a society to shy away from appropriating reasonable penalties for wrongdoing.

Now, to the practical: While we know that crime is rampant in this country—and that it has been rampant for decades—it is simply impossible to know how many *additional* crimes have been averted because the death penalty exists. I liken the phenomenon to the air-traffic-control system. Because an air-traffic controller works dutifully to provide order in the skies, untold numbers of lives are saved each and every day. But remove the air-traffic-control system all together, and I guarantee crashes would happen hundreds of times a day. We look to our judicial system to provide restraint, deterrence, order. Our society is far better, far *safer*, as a result.

—o-o-o—

The Welfare of the Criminal

A third and final consideration centers on the welfare of the criminal.

What if you knew you were going to die in the morning? I remember thinking about that question years ago, on the infamous day when Karla Faye Tucker was being put to death a few hours south of me, in Huntsville. I admired her courage and her obvious faith in Jesus, which was exhibited until she inhaled her final breath. Would I have been so courageous, if I had been the one facing death?

> Now is the time to be saved, for that "final day" is coming.

Hebrews 9:27 says, "It is appointed for man to die once, and after that comes judgment." We all will die. We all will face God's judgment. And, equally true, we all have an opportunity to surrender to the lordship of Christ now. *Now* is the time to be saved, for that "final day" is coming. And for the criminal about to be put to death, there is direct knowledge of that date. Oh, that they would allow that knowledge to spur them toward repentance! In this way, the government really does serve as God's "minister for good" … in many cases, even *ultimate* good.

Two distinct thoughts captured my attention, as I considered Karla Faye Tucker taking those slow steps into the death chamber, where she would be executed by lethal injection. The first was an acknowledgment of my own sinfulness, before a holy and perfect God: "There but by the grace of God go I."

And the second, a reaffirmation of my role in saving all the other little eight- and ten-year-old "Karla Faye Tuckers" who run the streets of our country today from an equally tragic end to their lives here on earth. Indeed, the best deterrent to crime is a changed heart. For those of us who love and serve the Lord Jesus, it is our responsibility to point as many people as possible to His saving grace.

> For those of us who love and serve the Lord Jesus, it is our responsibility to point as many people as possible to His saving grace.

In 1970, my own father was murdered, bludgeoned to death by a shoplifter, right there in the parking lot of Dad's

hardware store in Fort Worth, Texas. My dad survived
with the aid of heavy machinery for ten days' time in a
hospital bed, but when it became evident to my family and
me that Dad was not going to pull through, I ducked out
and went downstairs to the little hospital chapel, to spend
a few minutes alone with God. I got on my knees, shut my
tear-clouded eyes, and prayed to my heavenly Father for
added resolve to reach more and more people with His good
news. It was a twenty-four-year-old man who killed my dad,
just a wayward soul who made a series of bad choices one
day. "What if I had been able to reach him for Christ?" I
wondered, there between the pews of that chapel.

I recommitted myself to the work of evangelism, to spending
every single day God gave me telling men and women and
boys and girls about the magnificent love of Christ. Yes,
we must busy ourselves caring for those who are suffering
behind prison walls, caring for their needs, lifting them up
in prayer, expressing God's unwavering love for their souls.
But we must never neglect to do the work of *prevention*, by
proclaiming to all listening ears: "Jesus saves!"

postscript

As lovers of God, you and I are expected to live black-and-white lives in a very gray world. We are expected to uphold the banner of truth, even as lies swirl all around. We are expected to administer things like kindness and love and grace, while anger and vitriol are often doled out in return. And while these expectations may seem too high—too lofty—for everyday folks such as you and me, I promise you we are up to the task, with the power of God's Spirit working in our hearts.

I want to leave you with the image of a three-legged stool in mind, as you seek to live rightly in a wrong world. What follows are the legs of that stool that, when equally tended to, will keep you in beautiful balance.

Think Scripturally

First, *think scripturally*. Many Christians do not know their

Bibles and are therefore vulnerable to attacks from our enemy, who seeks to destroy our very lives. Refuse to live this way! Read your Bible. Know what you believe. Know why you believe what you believe. And defend that truth every day of your life.

> Read your Bible. Know what you believe. Know why you believe what you believe. And defend that truth every day of your life.

Live Purely

Second, *live purely*. God says in His Word, "Be holy for I am holy" (see 1 Peter 1:16), and it ought to be our daily goal to pursue godliness, holiness, and truth. We have the Spirit of Holy God living inside of us, enabling us to practice a lifestyle that is pleasing to God. Let's choose that lifestyle, shall we? Let's abandon the practice of inching closer and closer to the cultural fire, thinking, "Hmmm … I wonder if I'll get burned."

Let's maintain an innocence about sin and its consequences. Not naiveté, mind you, but a certain innocence that says, "I've not been contaminated by this world." Let's choose purity—of thought, of word, of deed. Let's *honor* God with the days of our lives.

Love Generously

Finally, *love generously*. We overcome evil with good, my friend. We overcome darkness with light. And we overcome apathy in all its awful forms with generous helpings of *love*. We may not be able to change Washington, D.C., overnight. We may not even be able to change dysfunctional dynamics in our own *home* overnight. But we can choose today to love well. Say a loving word. Extend a loving hand. Offer a loving gesture. Be known for your great love. As you love others, you show them the love of our Father. As you care deeply, you show them He cares.

Please call 1-800-414-7693 to order the following products:

books

A Man of God

Are You Fit for Life?

Courageous Parenting

Life According to Jesus

Lessons from the Heart

A Hope and a Future

Powering Up

Triumph! How You Can Overcome Death and Gain Eternal Life

The Promise of Persistent Prayer

devotionals

A Daily Encounter with God

booklets

30 Days to Powerful Prayer

The Truth About Influence

True Womanhood

God's Promises For Doubt-Filled Days

New Life in Christ (English and Spanish)

Rock Solid

Pause: Resting In God Instead of Stressing Out

Lifebook: The Authority, Authenticity and Accuracy of God's Word

G R A H A M

1-800-414-7693 (1-800-414-POWER)

jgraham@powerpoint.org

jackgraham.org